◇TELL ME ABOUT◇
EARTH, SEA & SKY

SERIES EDITOR: JACKIE GAFF

ILLUSTRATED BY CHRIS FORSEY

Kingfisher Books

Series editor: Jackie Gaff
Series designer: Terry Woodley

Author: Tom Stacy
Consultant: Terry Jennings
Illustrator: Chris Forsey
Editor: Louise Pritchard
Editorial assistant: Anne O'Daly

Kingfisher Books, Grisewood & Dempsey Ltd,
Elsley House, 24–30 Great Titchfield Street,
London W1P 7AD.

First published in 1990 by Kingfisher Books

BRITISH LIBRARY CATALOGUING IN PUBLICATION DATA
Gaff, Jackie
    Earth, sea and sky.
    1. Earth
    I. Title II. Forsey, Chris. III. Series
    550

ISBN 0 86272 556 9

Phototypeset by Southern Positives and Negatives
(SPAN), Lingfield, Surrey.
Printed in Spain.

Contents

What does the Earth look like?

If you could look at the Earth from Space, you would see it is spherical, or ball-shaped. It isn't completely round, though — it's slightly flattened at the Poles and it bulges at the Equator. The Earth looks very blue from Space because it is mostly covered with water.

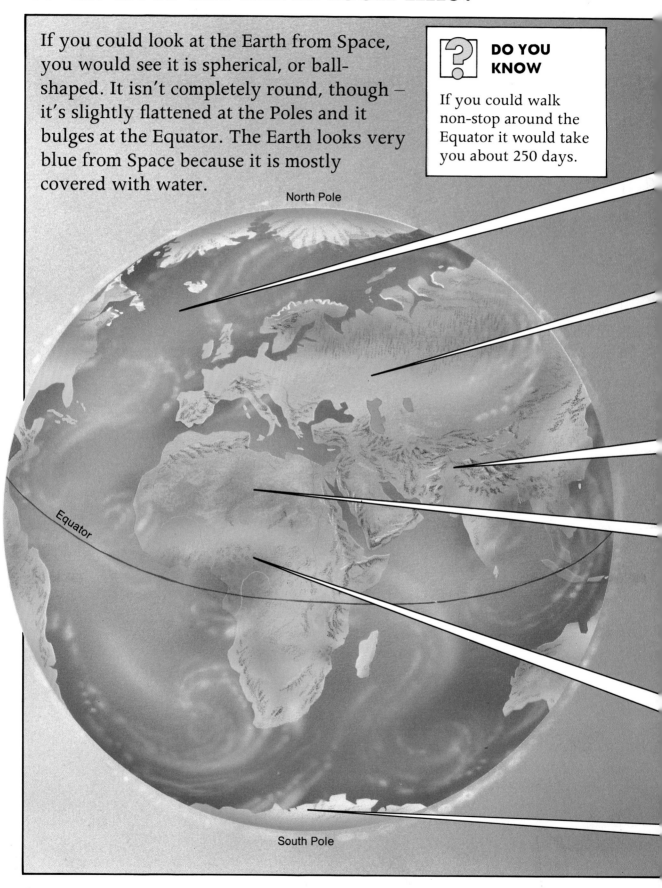

North Pole

Equator

South Pole

4

Water and ice cover seven-tenths of the Earth's surface.

Large areas of land are used for growing crops such as corn.

Mountains cover nearly one fifth of the Earth's land surface.

Nearly one eighth of the land area is dry desert.

Forests cover one quarter of the Earth's land surface. Parts are being cleared for villages and farms.

The Earth's coldest places are the North and South Poles.

 EARTH FACTS

● The Equator is an imaginary line around the Earth's middle which measures 40,091 km – it would take 25 million people holding hands to encircle it!

● The Equator divides the Earth into two equal halves called hemispheres. The top half is called the northern hemisphere. The bottom half is the southern hemisphere.

● An imaginary line through the centre of the Earth, from North Pole to South Pole, is called the Earth's axis. The Earth spins on its axis all the time, like a giant top.

● From North to South Poles – through the Earth's axis – measures 12,719 km.

What is inside the Earth?

The Earth is made of rock and has four main layers. We live on the surface skin, which is called the crust. The other layers are the mantle, and the outer and inner cores. It is very hot inside the Earth, and it gets hotter towards the middle – the temperature at the centre may be as much as 6000°C.

DO YOU KNOW

Scientists believe that the Earth and the Moon were both formed about 4600 million years ago. The oldest-known rocks on Earth were found in Canada in 1989 – they are more than 4000 million years old. Astronauts have discovered even older rocks on the Moon.

If the Earth were the size of an orange, its crust would be thinner than the orange's peel. Its thickness varies between 6 and 40 km.

The Earth's mantle is about 2900 km thick. The mantle is so hot that some of its rock is part-melted and moves slowly – a bit like treacle.

The outer core lies below the mantle. It is about 2000 km thick and very very hot – about 5000°C at its deepest – so hot that its rock is liquid.

Although it is so hot, the inner core of the Earth is solid because of the weight of the rocks on top. The inner core is about 1300 km thick.

How has the Earth changed?

Scientists think that millions of years ago all the land on Earth was joined together. It gradually broke apart to form the continents, which are still moving today. This is because the Earth's crust is made up of lots of pieces called plates, which drift on the thick half-melted rocks of the mantle. As the plates move, so do the continents.

DO YOU KNOW

North America and Europe move 2 cm or so farther apart every year – that's 1 metre every 50 years.

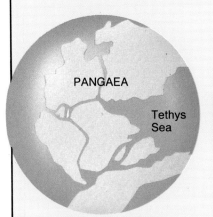

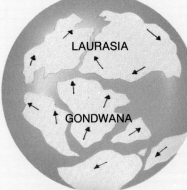

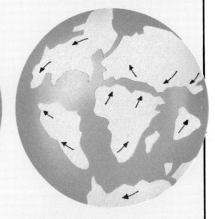

1 200 million years ago there was just one enormous land-mass. Scientists call this super-continent Pangaea. Around Pangaea was the Tethys Sea.

2 180 million years ago Pangaea split in two, as the plates beneath the Earth's crust moved. The continents that formed are called Laurasia and Gondwana.

3 65 million years ago Laurasia and Gondwana split into smaller continents. These moved farther apart and began to look like the continents of today.

MAKE AN EARTH JIGSAW

Trace the outlines of the continents from a map of the world on to paper. Cut out the shapes and see how the continents once fitted together.

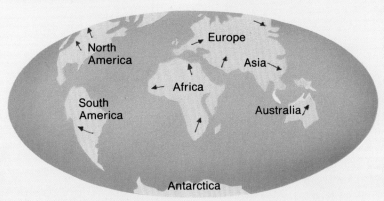

4 For more than 50 million years, Africa and South America have been moving apart at a rate of about 4 cm a year. The continents will continue to drift apart. 50 million years in the future, the Americas will have separated. Australia will have moved north, while Europe and Asia will have moved away from Africa.

How are mountains made?

It takes millions of years for mountains to form, and mountain building is still going on in parts of the Earth today. Some mountains form when rock is forced into folds by movements in the Earth's crust. Other mountains are made when whole blocks of rock are pushed up. Mountains can also be formed by volcanoes erupting.

Valleys form between two mountain peaks. Some were cut by icy glaciers or by fast-flowing rivers. Others were formed along faults in the Earth's crust.

Block mountains (left) form along breaks in the Earth's crust called faults. Huge blocks of rock are pushed up or tilted between faults. The Sierra Nevada in North America are block mountains.

Movement of rocks

The Alps in Europe are young fold mountains with sharp peaks. The American Appalachians are older, with worn rounded peaks.

A glacier is a mass of ice which moves slowly down a mountain, carving away the rock. Most glaciers only move 1 or 2 metres a day.

An avalanche is a sudden slip of snow and ice, which crashes down a mountain.

Movement of rocks

Fold mountains (above) are formed when parts of the Earth's crust bump and push against each other. Rock is squeezed up into folds, making new mountains.

MOUNTAIN FACTS

● Although the highest mountain is usually said to be Mount Everest, some people think another Himalayan mountain, K2, could be higher. The Himalayas are in Asia, between Tibet and Nepal.

● The first people to climb to the top of Mount Everest were Edmund Hillary and Tenzing Norgay in 1953.

● The world's 20 highest mountains are all in the Himalaya-Karakoram range. They are all over 8000 metres high.

● The highest peak in the Americas is Aconcagua in the Andes. It is 6960 metres high.

9

What is an earthquake?

When two plates in the Earth's crust push against one another, pressure builds up. If the strain becomes too great, the rocks move suddenly along faults and an earthquake happens.

In an earthquake, the ground trembles for several seconds and wide cracks can appear in it. Buildings shake and sometimes collapse. Scientists know where earthquakes are likely, but they cannot yet tell exactly when they will happen.

EARTHQUAKE FACTS

● The most destructive earthquake ever recorded happened in Japan in 1923. More than 575,000 houses were destroyed.

● In an earthquake in China in 1556, more than 800,000 people were killed. Around 25,000 people are thought to have died in the 1988 earthquake in Armenia.

● The strength of an earthquake is measured on the Richter scale. The strongest earthquake measured so far was 8.9 on the Richter scale. The 1989 San Francisco quake registered 6.9.

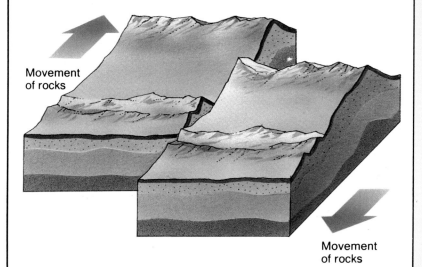

Movement of rocks

Movement of rocks

What is a volcano?

A volcano is an opening in the Earth's crust which happens when the crust is being stretched or squeezed. When a volcano erupts, molten rock, burning gas and ash explode through the opening from deep inside the Earth.

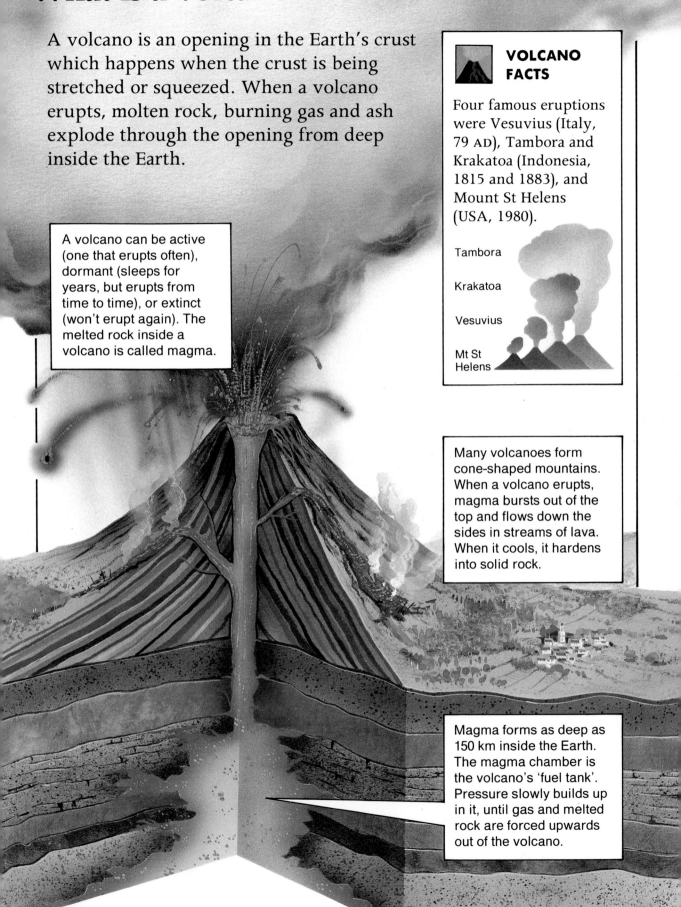

A volcano can be active (one that erupts often), dormant (sleeps for years, but erupts from time to time), or extinct (won't erupt again). The melted rock inside a volcano is called magma.

VOLCANO FACTS

Four famous eruptions were Vesuvius (Italy, 79 AD), Tambora and Krakatoa (Indonesia, 1815 and 1883), and Mount St Helens (USA, 1980).

Tambora

Krakatoa

Vesuvius

Mt St Helens

Many volcanoes form cone-shaped mountains. When a volcano erupts, magma bursts out of the top and flows down the sides in streams of lava. When it cools, it hardens into solid rock.

Magma forms as deep as 150 km inside the Earth. The magma chamber is the volcano's 'fuel tank'. Pressure slowly builds up in it, until gas and melted rock are forced upwards out of the volcano.

How are rocks made?

There are three main kinds of rock – igneous, sedimentary and metamorphic. Each kind was made in a different way and may have taken many thousands of years to form. All rocks contain materials called minerals.

ROCK FACTS

● Chalk is a sedimentary rock. It is made up of the shells of tiny sea creatures which lived many millions of years ago.

● Pumice is a type of igneous rock which is so light that it will float in water.

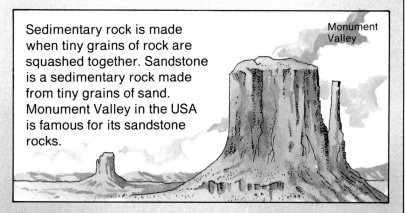

Sedimentary rock is made when tiny grains of rock are squashed together. Sandstone is a sedimentary rock made from tiny grains of sand. Monument Valley in the USA is famous for its sandstone rocks.

Monument Valley

Metamorphic, or changed rock, is made deep underground when heat and pressure alter another kind of rock. Marble is a metamorphic rock often used in building and by sculptors. It was formed from limestone.

Michelangelo's Pietà

Igneous, or fiery, rock was once liquid, deep inside the Earth. Then it cooled and hardened on or below the Earth's surface. The Giant's Causeway in Ireland is made of an igneous rock called basalt.

Giant's Causeway

What are stalactites and stalagmites?

Stalactites and stalagmites form inside limestone caves. They are made by drips of water which contain a mineral called calcite. As the water dries up, the calcite slowly builds into a column.

Stalactites grow from the roof of a cave, stalagmites from the cave floor. They sometimes meet to form a pillar.

MAKE YOUR OWN STALACTITES

1 Fill two glass jars with warm water. Wearing rubber gloves to protect your hands, make a solution by stirring in washing soda until no more will dissolve.

2 Weight the ends of a twisted wool thread and dip one in each jar. Place a saucer between the jars, beneath the thread.

3 Tiny stalactites will grow, as soda dries out from solution carried up the wool.

Where do rivers start?

There would be no rivers without rain, snow and ice. Some of this water soaks into the ground, where it collects and is called ground water. Sometimes it bubbles up out of the ground again as a spring and starts a stream. The stream cuts out a channel, or path, for itself and grows wider to form a river. The river gets larger as other streams join it, until finally it reaches the sea.

 DO YOU KNOW

The Colorado River has taken millions of years to cut the Grand Canyon in the USA. This is the world's largest gorge.

A river is often joined by smaller rivers. These are called tributaries. They make the river larger.

2 When it reaches flat lowlands, the river is wider. It slowly meanders, or bends.

3 Near the sea the river is wide. At its estuary, or mouth, its fresh water mingles with sea water.

As a river slows down, it drops mud and bits of rock it is carrying. Some rivers create huge fan-shapes of mud and rock at their mouths. These are called deltas.

1 Young rivers flow quickly downhill and may cut deep gorges in the rock.

Water can be stored behind a dam and used to drive machines to make electricity.

A canal is a river cut through the land by people, for ships and barges to travel along.

RIVER FACTS

● The world's longest river is the Nile. It is 6670 km long.

AFRICA

Nile

● At 6437 km, the Amazon River in South America is the world's second longest river.

● The largest delta is that of the Ganges and Brahamputra rivers in Asia (75,000 sq km).

How are waterfalls made?

●The Niagara Falls (between Canada and the USA) are actually two falls – the Horseshoe and the American falls.

● The falls with the most water are the Boyoma Falls in Africa.

● The highest waterfall is the Angel Falls in South America, at 979 metres. This is twice as high as the tallest office building, the Sears Tower in Chicago, USA.

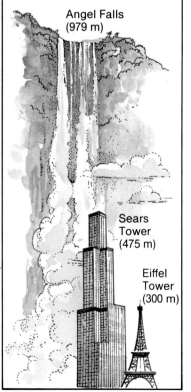

Angel Falls (979 m)

Sears Tower (475 m)

Eiffel Tower (300 m)

When a river flows over bands of hard and soft rock, the rushing water wears the soft rock away more quickly than it does the hard rock. This makes a ledge, over which the river begins to fall. Most waterfalls form in mountains, where rivers flow fastest and have more power to wear away the rock.

1

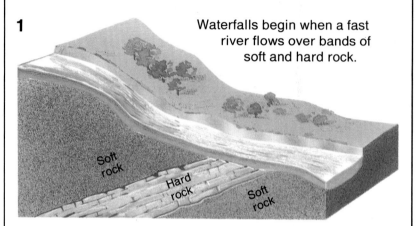

Waterfalls begin when a fast river flows over bands of soft and hard rock.

Soft rock

Hard rock

Soft rock

2

The water wears the soft rock away more quickly than the hard rock. A ledge forms, and the water falls over it.

3

Over thousands of years, the water wears away more rock and the waterfall gets bigger and bigger.

How are lakes made?

Most natural lakes form when a river is blocked by rocks or ice which dam a valley. Melting glaciers leave behind large amounts of rock, and this often makes a dam. Water then fills the valley to form a lake. Other lakes are made when rivers change course.

LAKE FACTS

● The world's largest lake is the Caspian Sea, in Asia. It covers 372,000 sq km. The deepest is Lake Baikal in the USSR, with a depth of 1620 metres.

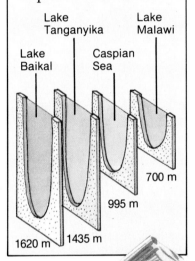

Lake Tanganyika

Lake Malawi

Lake Baikal

Caspian Sea

1620 m   1435 m   995 m   700 m

As it moves, a glacier cuts a deep valley out of the rock. It pushes boulders ahead of it, which form a dam when the glacier melts away.

Slow rivers drop much of the mud and sand they are carrying. In time their path is blocked. They change course, leaving a lake in the old bend.

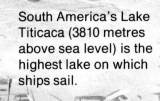

South America's Lake Titicaca (3810 metres above sea level) is the highest lake on which ships sail.

How deep are the oceans?

OCEAN FACTS

- The Pacific Ocean covers 165,200,000 sq km – a larger area than all the continents put together.

- The Atlantic is the second biggest ocean. It covers 81,660,000 sq km. Its deepest point is the Puerto Rico Trench in the West Indies, at nearly 9000 metres.

- The world's deepest place is the Mariana Trench in the Pacific. Over 11,000 metres deep, it could swallow Mount Everest.

Metres

1000	
2000	
3000	
4000	
5000	Mariana Trench
6000	
7000	
8000	
9000	
10,000	
11,000	

The world's biggest and deepest ocean is the Pacific. Its lowest point is the bottom of the Mariana Trench, which is over 11,000 metres deep. However, most of the ocean floor is a flat plain called the abyss, which is about 4000 metres deep. The maximum depth of the Atlantic Ocean is nearly 9000 metres, and of the Indian Ocean, nearly 8000 metres.

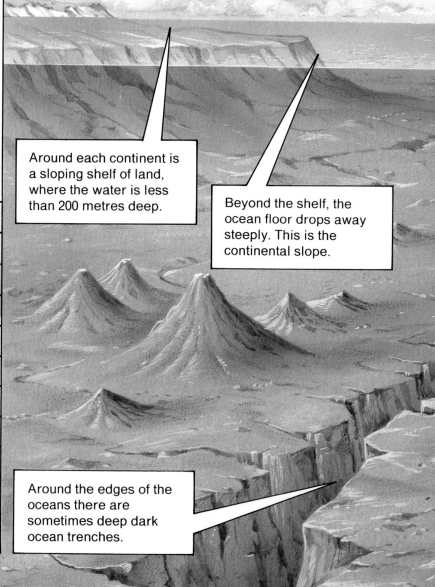

Around each continent is a sloping shelf of land, where the water is less than 200 metres deep.

Beyond the shelf, the ocean floor drops away steeply. This is the continental slope.

Around the edges of the oceans there are sometimes deep dark ocean trenches.

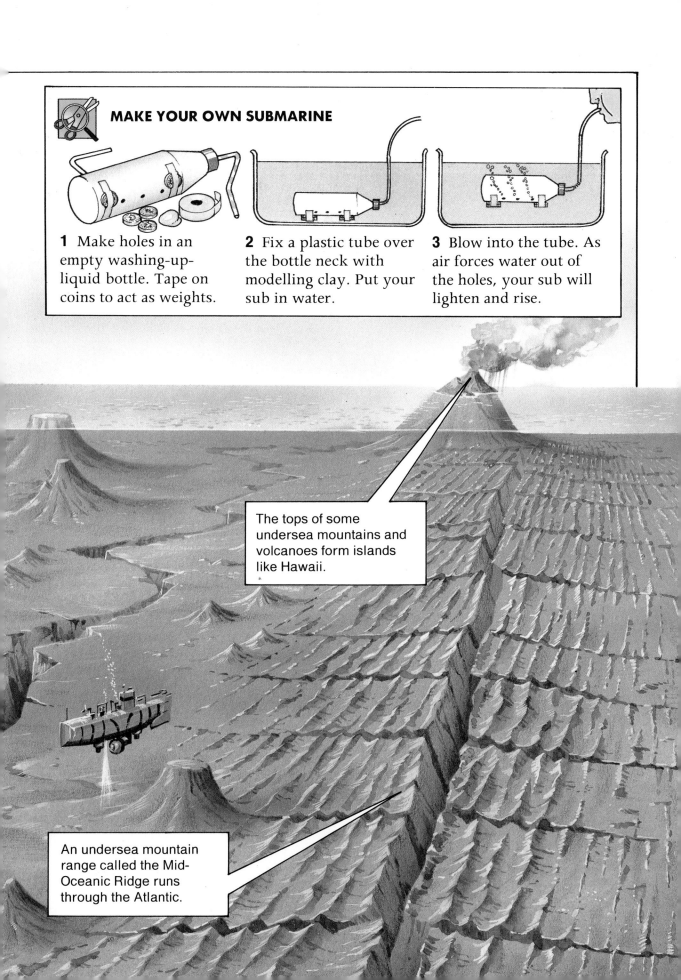

MAKE YOUR OWN SUBMARINE

1 Make holes in an empty washing-up-liquid bottle. Tape on coins to act as weights.

2 Fix a plastic tube over the bottle neck with modelling clay. Put your sub in water.

3 Blow into the tube. As air forces water out of the holes, your sub will lighten and rise.

The tops of some undersea mountains and volcanoes form islands like Hawaii.

An undersea mountain range called the Mid-Oceanic Ridge runs through the Atlantic.

Why is the sea salty?

The salt in the sea is a mixture of minerals, which dissolve from rocks on land and wash into the sea. These minerals make the sea taste salty. They include the salt we eat, which is called sodium chloride.

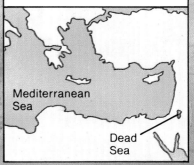

Mediterranean Sea

Dead Sea

What are the highest waves?

The highest ocean wave ever recorded measured 34 metres. It was seen during a Pacific Ocean hurricane in 1933. Ocean waves are caused mainly by the wind and the pull of the Sun and Moon.

What are icebergs?

Icebergs are huge blocks of ice which break off the ends of glaciers and drift out to sea. They are found in the polar regions – the Arctic in the north and the Antarctic in the south. Icebergs drift towards warmer waters, often travelling thousands of kilometres and lasting for several years before finally melting.

The tallest iceberg ever seen was 167 metres high. The biggest was 335 km long and 97 km across.

Antarctic icebergs like these are long and flat-topped – they look like floating islands of ice. In the Arctic, icebergs are usually tall and an uneven shape.

ICEBERG FACTS

● Blown by the wind, an iceberg can 'sail' at almost 2 km/h.

● Not all icebergs are white. Some are brown, others are black or green.

● Only about one eighth of an iceberg shows above water.

21

What is the atmosphere?

The atmosphere is the air that surrounds the Earth. Without it there would be no life on our planet, as it contains the oxygen we breathe and it protects us from the Sun's strong rays. The atmosphere gets thinner higher up and ends about 500 km above the Earth. This is where Space begins.

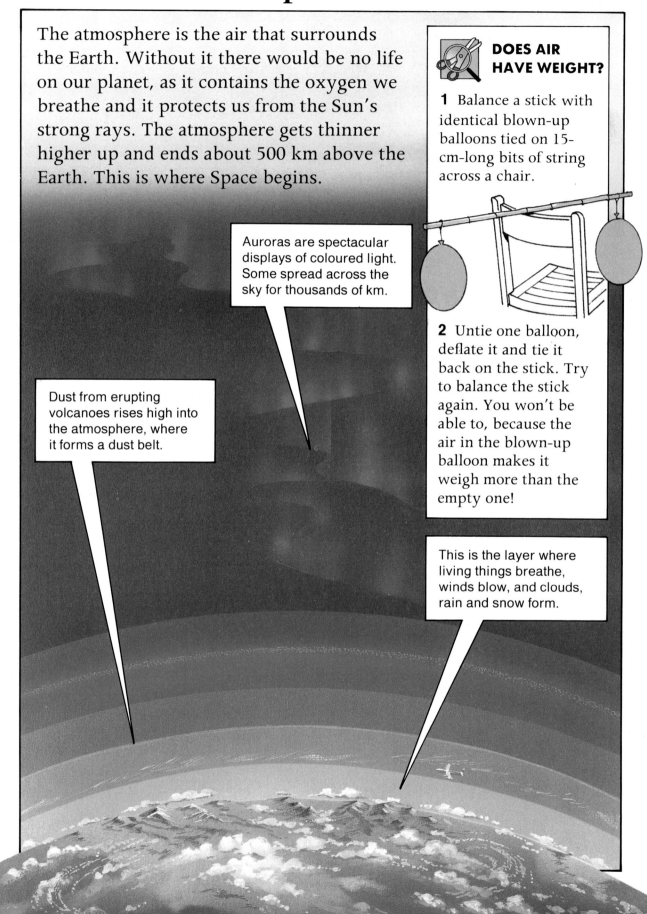

Auroras are spectacular displays of coloured light. Some spread across the sky for thousands of km.

Dust from erupting volcanoes rises high into the atmosphere, where it forms a dust belt.

DOES AIR HAVE WEIGHT?

1 Balance a stick with identical blown-up balloons tied on 15-cm-long bits of string across a chair.

2 Untie one balloon, deflate it and tie it back on the stick. Try to balance the stick again. You won't be able to, because the air in the blown-up balloon makes it weigh more than the empty one!

This is the layer where living things breathe, winds blow, and clouds, rain and snow form.

Why is the sky blue?

Sunlight looks white, but it is really a mixture of the colours you see in rainbows. When light rays from the Sun reach the Earth's atmosphere, they are scattered by tiny bits of dust and water in the air. Blue light gets scattered the most and we see it from all angles. That's why the sky looks blue.

Why are sunsets red?

At sunset, the Sun is low in the sky and farther away from us. Its light has to pass through more air before it reaches our eyes. This extra air scatters out all the colours except red. Only red rays reach our eyes and we see a red sunset.

? DO YOU KNOW

At midsummer in the Arctic and Antarctic the Sun never sets. It's known as the Midnight Sun.

Why do we have seasons?

We have seasons because of the way the Earth orbits, or travels round, the Sun. The Earth is tilted on its axis, and during the year of its orbit different parts get stronger or weaker sunlight, because they are closer or farther from the Sun. When the northern hemisphere is tilted towards the Sun, for example, that part of the Earth has summer.

 SUNLIGHT FACTS

The Sun's rays have to travel farther to get to the Poles than to reach the Equator. The rays have less heat left, and that's why the Poles are so cold.

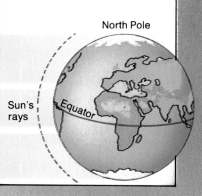

North Pole

Sun's rays

Equator

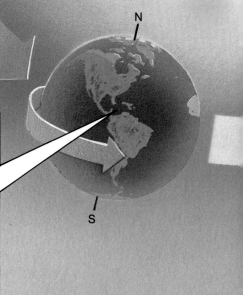

N

Summer in northern hemisphere

S

Winter in southern hemisphere

N

S

In autumn in the northern hemisphere, animals prepare for winter.

In the southern hemisphere, spring comes and birds begin to nest.

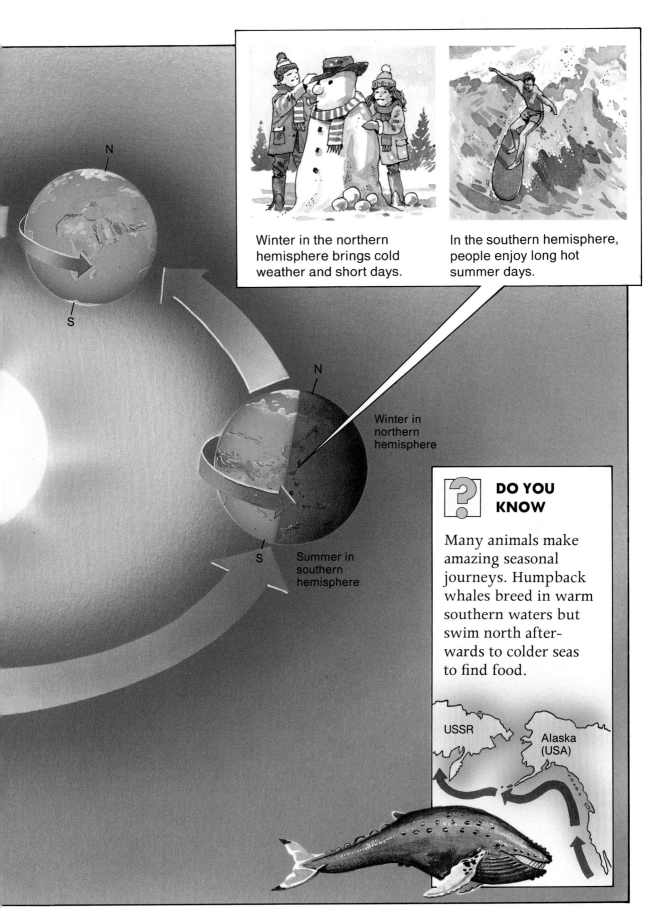

Winter in the northern hemisphere brings cold weather and short days.

In the southern hemisphere, people enjoy long hot summer days.

N

S

N

Winter in northern hemisphere

S

Summer in southern hemisphere

DO YOU KNOW

Many animals make amazing seasonal journeys. Humpback whales breed in warm southern waters but swim north afterwards to colder seas to find food.

USSR

Alaska (USA)

Why do we have day and night?

The Earth is spinning round while it orbits the Sun – one complete spin takes 24 hours. It is light during the day, and dark at night, because the Sun's rays only reach the half of the Earth that is turned towards it. The half that is facing the Sun has day. The half that is facing away from the Sun is in shadow. There it is night.

MAKE DAY AND NIGHT

You need a globe for the Earth, and a torch for the Sun. Make a room dark and rest the torch on a table so that it shines on half the globe. Slowly spin the globe. As it spins round, each part of your 'Earth' will move through 'day-time' into 'night-time'.

The central line on which something spins is called its axis. The Earth's axis passes through the Poles and is tilted slightly.

Why are days different lengths?

At the Equator, day and night are roughly the same length all year round. Towards the Poles, however, winter days are shorter than summer days. This is because the Earth is tilted on its axis. When part of the Earth is tilted away from the Sun it has shorter days, because it has less time within reach of the Sun's rays.

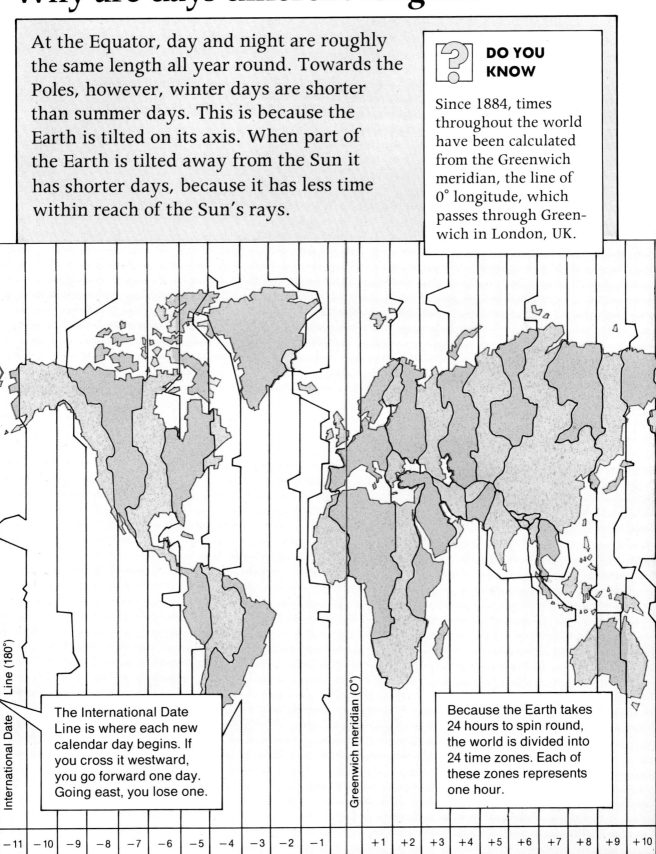

DO YOU KNOW

Since 1884, times throughout the world have been calculated from the Greenwich meridian, the line of 0° longitude, which passes through Greenwich in London, UK.

International Date Line (180°)

Greenwich meridian (0°)

The International Date Line is where each new calendar day begins. If you cross it westward, you go forward one day. Going east, you lose one.

Because the Earth takes 24 hours to spin round, the world is divided into 24 time zones. Each of these zones represents one hour.

| −11 | −10 | −9 | −8 | −7 | −6 | −5 | −4 | −3 | −2 | −1 | | +1 | +2 | +3 | +4 | +5 | +6 | +7 | +8 | +9 | +10 |

HOURS

Where are the hottest places?

The highest temperature ever measured in the shade was 58°C in the Sahara Desert of North Africa, in September 1922. It was nearly as hot at Death Valley in the USA in July 1913, when the temperature reached 56.7°C. The Earth is hottest near the Equator, as this is always roughly the same distance from the Sun and receives its strongest rays.

Where are the coldest places?

The world's coldest places are near the North and South Poles. The Sun never rises very high in the sky there, and its rays are weak. Snow and ice cover the ground all year round.

The lowest temperature on record is -89.2°C. This was reached in July 1983, at Vostok, a Soviet base in Antarctica.

Where are the wettest places?

Tutunendo in Colombia, South America, has an average of more than 11,000 mm of rain a year. This makes it the world's wettest place. But Cherrapunji in India holds the record for having the most rain in a month – 9300 mm in July 1861. That year it had more than 26,000 mm of rain! On Mount Wai-'ale-'ale in Hawaii, it rains on 350 out of the 365 days in the year.

DO YOU KNOW

The three wettest countries are near the Equator. They are Colombia in South America, Malaysia in Asia, and Sierra Leone in Africa.

Where are the driest places?

The driest place in the world is the Atacama Desert in northern Chile, South America. Until 1971, it had not rained there for 400 years! The world's driest country is Egypt, which has large areas of desert.

All deserts are dry, although not all are hot and sandy. Some are cold, and some are rocky or gravelly.

DO YOU KNOW

The eastern Sahara Desert in North Africa has over 4000 hours of sunshine a year – that's nearly 11 hours each day. This makes it the world's sunniest place.

What makes the wind blow?

The wind is just air masses of different temperatures moving. The Sun heats up different parts of the land and sea, which then warm the air above them. The warm air rises because it is lighter than cold air. As it does, cold air moves in to take its place as a cold wind. Similarly, heavy cold air sinks and warm air flows in to take its place as a warm wind.

Air warmed over the land rises. Cold air from the sea pushes in beneath it, as a cold wind.

MAKE A WIND VANE

1 Glue triangles of card into slits at either end of a drinking straw, to make an arrow.

2 Take a pencil with an eraser on the end and use modelling clay to fix it through the hole in an upturned flowerpot.

3 Pin the arrow to the pencil eraser, making sure the straw can move round freely.

4 Use chalk to mark compass points on the pot. Put your wind vane outdoors to see where the wind is blowing from.

What is a hurricane?

Hurricanes are violent tropical storms in which the wind spirals round at speeds of more than 120 km/h. They begin over the ocean, when warm moist air rises very quickly and cooler air rushes in below. The air spirals, getting faster and faster.

If a hurricane reaches land it can do great damage. Once over land, however, away from the ocean conditions that cause it, the storm begins to die down.

STORM FACTS

● A hurricane is usually about 300 km across, but some are over 500 km across. The eye measures about 15 km.

● Tornadoes form over land. They are smaller than hurricanes, and last less time, but they are much stronger.

The centre of a hurricane is called the eye. The air is calm here, but all around the eye of the hurricane the winds whirl with terrifying force.

What are clouds made of?

Clouds are made up of millions of tiny water droplets. They form when moist air rises, or when warm and cold air meet. This makes a gas called water vapour in the air cool and become liquid again. In all, there are about ten different types of cloud.

Cirrus clouds are thin and wispy. They form above 10,000 metres and can signal rain.

Altocumulus look like a pile of small greyish-white clouds jumbled together.

Cirrocumulus are high ice clouds which warn that the weather is going to be cold.

Stratocumulus is a lumpy sheet of rounded clouds which may bring light falls of rain.

Stratus are low thick sheets of fog-like cloud covering the sky. They often bring drizzle.

Nimbostratus clouds form a smooth layer of grey across the sky. They bring rain or snow.

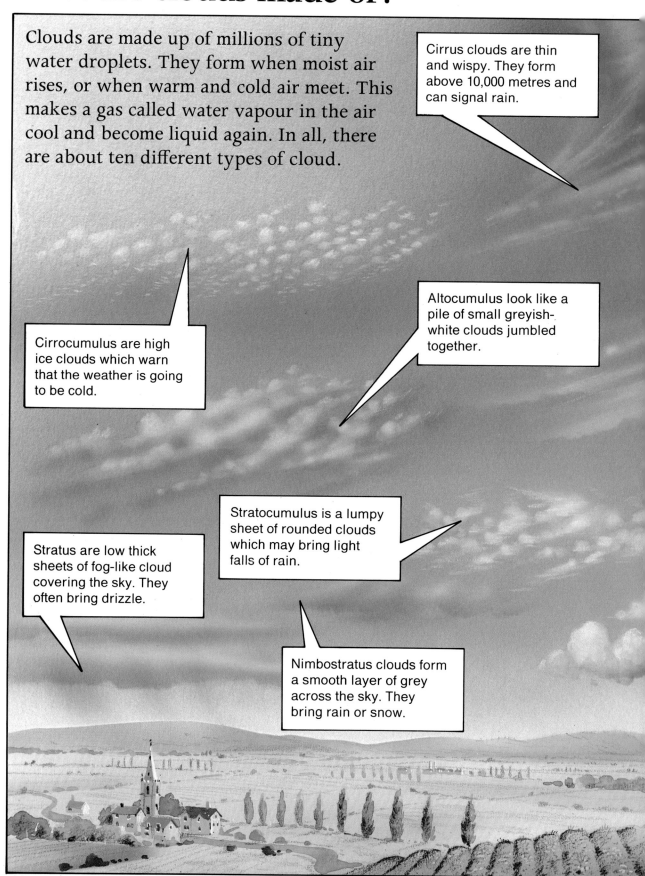

Cirrostratus clouds are high and hazy. They can mean that rain or snow is on the way.

Altostratus clouds form a thin grey or white layer across the sky. They warn of rain.

Cumulonimbus clouds can tower 20,000 metres into the sky. They produce rain, snow, hail or thunderstorms.

Cumulus clouds form in fluffy white heaps. Small ones are a sign of fine weather on the way.

THUNDER FACTS

● Lightning is a giant electric spark which flashes from cloud to cloud or to the ground in a storm.

● When air is heated by a flash of lightning, it expands very quickly, making the noise called thunder. Light travels much faster than sound, so we always see the lightning before we hear the thunder.

● You can tell how many kilometres away a storm is by counting the seconds between a lightning flash and the thunder, then dividing by three.

Why does it rain?

Rain happens when clouds cool. All clouds are made from water droplets, which form when the water vapour in air cools and becomes liquid again. The higher a cloud rises, the more water it carries. The droplets get bigger and heavier until they are too heavy to float and they fall as rain. Each droplet collects smaller droplets as it falls, until the final raindrop is several thousand times its original size.

DO YOU KNOW

Raindrops are round with a flattened base – not tear-shaped, as they are often drawn.

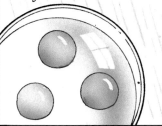

MAKE A RAIN GAUGE

1 Rain gauges are used to measure rainfall. To make your own, stick a piece of paper on a straight-sided jar.

2 Pour 200 ml of water into the jar, 10 ml at a time. Mark the level for each 10 ml on the paper.

3 Empty the jar and put a funnel in its mouth. Put your gauge outside to catch the rain.

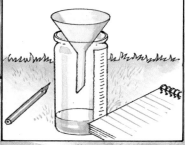

Why do rainbows form?

Although sunlight looks white, it is really made up of several colours. When the Sun's rays pass through raindrops, this separates sunlight into its different colours and a rainbow forms.

Rainbows are really complete circles, but on Earth we can only see half of them. To see one, you must have the Sun behind you at a fairly low angle in the sky.

 DO YOU KNOW

High up in an aircraft you might be able to see a rainbow as a complete circle.

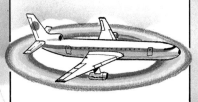

MAKE A RAINBOW

1 Put a bowl of water in bright sunlight. Rest a flat mirror inside the bowl to catch the light.

2 Put some white card in front of the bowl. Adjust the mirror until you can see a rainbow on the card.

White light is made up of red, orange, yellow, green, blue, indigo and violet light.

White light

Raindrop

Why are snowflakes different shapes?

No two snowflakes have exactly the same pattern, but if you could look at them under a microscope you would see that they all have either six sides or six points. Snowflakes form when the temperature drops and the water vapour in very cold clouds freezes into crystals of ice.

SNOW AND ICE FACTS

● Nine-tenths of the world's ice is in Antarctica, where the ice sheet can be as much as 4800 metres thick.

● The most snow ever to fall in one snowstorm is 4800 mm. This happened in California, USA, in 1921.

● Snow contains less water than rain. It takes 250 ml of melted dry snow to give as much water as 25 ml of rain.

What is hail?

Hailstones form in cold weather, when water droplets freeze at the top of storm-clouds. The droplets start to fall, but air currents lift them to the top of the clouds again and a new layer of ice is added. The hailstones get bigger and heavier, until finally they fall to Earth.

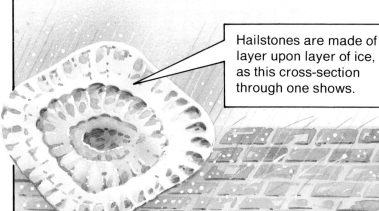

Hailstones are made of layer upon layer of ice, as this cross-section through one shows.

 DO YOU KNOW

The largest hailstone on record fell in 1970. It was 19 cm across – almost as big as a soccer ball. The heaviest hailstone weighed just over 1 kg and fell in 1986.

What are dew and frost?

Dew forms on clear still nights, when water vapour in the air cools into water droplets. We see it in the morning, as beads of water on plants and on spider's webs. When the temperature falls below 0°C, the dew freezes – frost is frozen dew.

 DO YOU KNOW

In some cold regions, the ground is frozen all year round. In Siberia, USSR, this frozen layer (called permafrost) is more than 600 metres thick.

What is the greenhouse effect?

Greenhouses are warm because their glass lets sunlight through, but stops warm air escaping. A layer of carbon dioxide and other gases in the atmosphere is doing the same thing to the Earth. It lets the Sun's rays through, but stops most of the heat from the Earth escaping back into Space. This is called the greenhouse effect and it is making the Earth hotter and hotter.

Carbon dioxide gas is made when oil, coal, natural gas and wood are burnt as fuel.

DO YOU KNOW

If the Earth goes on warming, the polar ice caps will melt. Sea levels will rise and flood low-lying land.

Useful words

Atmosphere The air that surrounds the Earth. It is largely made up of the gases nitrogen and oxygen, but also has water vapour, dust and small amounts of other gases in it.

Axis An imaginary straight line through the centre of the Earth from North Pole to South Pole. The Earth spins on its axis while it orbits the Sun.

Continent Continents are large areas of land, and the Earth has seven of them – Africa, Antarctica, Asia, Australia, Europe, North America and South America.

Core The centre of the Earth.

Crust The Earth has four main layers. Working from the outside in, these are the crust, the mantle, the outer core and the inner core.

Equator An imaginary line around the Earth, halfway between the North and South Poles. The Equator divides the Earth into two equal parts called hemispheres.

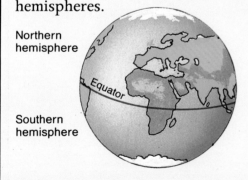

Northern hemisphere

Equator

Southern hemisphere

Fault A break or line of weakness in the Earth's crust.

Hemisphere One half of the Earth. The Northern Hemisphere is above the Equator, and the Southern Hemisphere is below it.

Latitude and Longitude Lines of latitude and longitude are drawn on maps of the world. Latitude lines run from East to West, and longitude lines run from North to South. They are measured in degrees. The Equator is 0° latitude, for example.

Mantle One of the four main layers of the Earth. The mantle is the layer below the Earth's surface, and it is made up of part-melted rock.

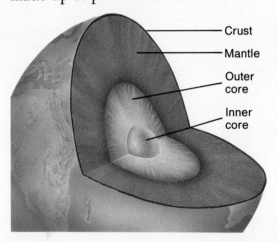

Crust

Mantle

Outer core

Inner core

Mineral Any natural material found in the ground that doesn't come from plants or animals. All rocks are made up of minerals, for example. There are about 2500 types of mineral, including copper, gold, silver and diamond.

Orbit The curved path of something that travels around a star or a planet. The Earth travels around the Sun (a star) in an orbit, for example.

Pole The Earth has two Poles. The North Pole is at the top of the Earth and the South Pole is at the bottom.

Water vapour Water is usually a liquid, but it can also be a solid (ice) or a gas. When water is a gas it is called water vapour.

Index